The Fallacies of Atheism

by

C. P. Klapper

Also by C. P. Klapper

~

The Washington Poems
Sonnets for the Spanish

The Fallacies of Atheism

by

C. P. Klapper

The Lion and Lambda Press
Metuchen, NJ

ISBN-13: 978-1-934882-03-0 (paperback)

Library of Congress Control Number: 2012918354

Printed in the United States of America.

Dedication

To all those I love

whatever their beliefs might be

Preface

I often find myself these days the odd man out. Whatever topic is being discussed in the great public forums, handsomely bifurcated into pro and con, my own thoughts are not on the one side or the other. That is, perhaps, to be expected of a poet. Our lot is one with the prophets, that we are ignored by the powerful and misunderstood by those they control. As the powerful and the controlled each set a pace in their deep tracks, they never care to question why the track is laid where it is while they dispute which direction to go down it. Any cares for the design of the debate – the positioning of the tracks of thought – they leave to poets of the past, reciting verses against each other in place of argument, as if their cherished set of proverbs are manifestly superior to those of their disputants.

So it is that I have been working on several books, presenting my views from above the tracks, when the topic of religion came into vogue, curiously brought to the fore by atheists. Less curiously, this discussion has been colored by the pejorative cant of atheism so that I feel myself called upon to put my current projects aside for the moment and share my own perspective and understanding on religion.

The reader might suppose from the title that I have prejudged all that comes from the atheist camp, but they would be wrong. There are many truths, and one key one, that comes from the atheists. The faithful would do well to consider those, if they have not already. However, for all the truths that come from the atheists, atheism itself is not one of them.

C. P. Klapper
Metuchen, NJ

Table of Contents

The Fallacy of Its Name

I t should be clear to anyone of faith that there is in the arguments of the self-proclaimed "atheist" a confusion of terms. Certainly, anyone who has felt the warm, white gleam of Love will not find in the straw man "god" posited by such "atheists" anything remotely corresponding to their own personal experience. Yet, rhetorical devices aside, there is a more fundamental and logical error made by these "atheists" embedded in the name they have chosen for their belief.

That name, "atheism", is defined as "the theory or belief that God does not exist"[1]. That definition thus depends for its meaning on the definition of "God". In order to avoid the "straw man" error, the definition of "God" necessarily has to be the modern definition used

---

1   Frank R. Abate, editor in chief, U. S. Dictionaries, *The Pocket Oxford American Dictionary of Current English*, (New York: Oxford University Press, 2002), p. 42.

by people of faith when they reason philosophically about their faith. What is at issue is not the emotional reasoning in communities of faith, though this forms the basis of faith. Religions are not debating societies, just as families, despite dinner table debates, are not debating societies. An entire dimension of religious intellect must be taken off the table when determining the definition of "God" in the context of the definition of "atheism". Yet that determination removes from a definition of "God" much of the disagreement amongst religions as to the nature of God. Instead, we can first elicit a definition of small-"g" "god" and, from that, determine a correct, albeit semantically poor definition of capital-"G" "God". Thus, though this limitation may seem crippling to the side of religion, in the biased view which many "atheists" hold of people of faith, it allows greater clarity within the universe of discourse. We can, at least, be speaking the same language.

In modern parlance, a "god" is something which is worshiped. Its synonym, "idol", conveys the same meaning. We speak metaphorically of "teen idols" and "guitar gods", of "worshiping" money, but the meaning is clearly based on "worship", whose etymology reveals the attribute of being "worthy". A "god" is therefore something which is of great worth to someone. Disputes as to the worthiness of someone's "god" lead to charges that they are worshiping a "false god". Because "idol" is used to denote the depiction of a worthy thing, as opposed to the worthy thing itself, it is also used in this pejorative sense of being a false god. This is reflected in the fact that, in English, we have no capital-"I" "Idol" synonymous to capital-"G" "God". The capitalization denotes universality, which is why there is so much disagreement over the nature of "God".

There is, however, no disagreement over that universality of worthiness being the fundamental definition of "God". The derived definition for modern use proceeds from derived meanings of "worth". That is, modern people of faith have reached some consensus on the notion of universal "worth". The basis of that consensus is ancient, as can be seen in the distinction between "false gods" and the "one true God". The key idea is that of "truth", not only in true universality and true worthiness, but in the truth embedded in the notion of "worth".

For from time immemorial, the worth of a thing has rested on how true it was in the context of what it was presumed to be. The worth of gold is based on the degree to which a golden thing is truly gold. If there are parts which are not gold, then they are false in that context and therefore worthless. A more ancient example would be water. Brackish water is composed of true water and the "not water" of salt. Cloudy water has parts which have the "not water" of sediment. Salt and sediment, which are true in their own context, are false in the context of water. We express the concept of "truth", when used in this manner, as "purity", complete truth being "pure", as in "pure gold" or "pure water". This sense is seen in purity codes and in animals which are pure, without blemish, being required for sacrifice. The expression "cleanliness is next to godliness" comes from the same notion, the dirt on your body being false in the context of you.

Turning now to the context, it is the identity or existence of the thing, though that was expressed more commonly with a name or with the verb "to be". Truth of existence, or "essence", is therefore the "worthiness" of any thing. The essence of all things would then be capital "E" "Existence", as this denotes the "existence" property in its purest and truest sense. This "Existence" is, by being the essence of all things, the universality of worthiness and therefore a derived definition of "God". One deeply rooted use of this definition of "God" is found in the name of God given in Exodus 3:14, which we translate as "I AM THAT I AM" and from which we get "Yahweh" and "Jehovah", as well as the name "Joshua" – meaning "Yahweh Saves" – and its variant "Jesus".

Even in and of itself, the notion of "God" as "Existence", derived from the concept of "worship", is necessarily monotheistic. This further confirms that in a world where the major religions are monotheistic, and assert that their one God is the true God, the operative definition of "God" is "Existence". This definition is therefore the only one which can be used to define "atheism".

"Atheism" is therefore "The theory or belief that Existence does not exist" or, equivalently "The theory or belief that there is no Existence". If, however, there is no capital-"E" "Existence", then there is no little-"e" "existence", that is, no existence for anything at all. Put another way, we might disagree about the nature of this essential "existentiality", but if we dispute that there is any such "existentiality" we are disputing whether there is anything with the property of existence. "Atheism" is therefore "The theory or belief that nothing exists". This is a more extreme position than "nihilism", which only posits that there is no meaning to existence. The name of this so-called "atheism" implies that such a philosophy does not itself exist.

Since the name "atheism" is self-contradictory when "God" is properly defined, that name is itself a "straw man" fallacy. We are thus left to deduce their actual philosophy from their appeals to ridicule, only noting in passing that those appeals are themselves fallacies. One likely candidate is materialism, given that they often use the words "supernatural" and "magical" pejoratively in such appeals and claim that they only use physical data to reach their own conclusions. We therefore turn next to the fallacy of materialism.

The Fallacy of Materialism

Materialism has been defined as "a theory that physical matter is the only or fundamental reality and that all being and processes and phenomena can be explained as manifestations or results of matter."[1] This may sound like an explicit definition, but there is an ambiguity in the words "physical" and "matter" which is resolved differently for common than for philosophical usage, leading to greater acceptance than is warranted. Also, "being" is listed with "processes" and "phenomena", so that "being" is presumed material by association with entities which are material in the common usage.

This ambiguity can be more consistently resolved by restating the definition with the word

---

1   Merriam-Webster Dictionary

"concrete", thus: "A theory that only the concrete exists." The "material" in this second definition of "materialism" is the philosophical usage of "concrete" and not the less precise common usage which allows for abstractions like "structure" in its "physical matter". The rest of the first definition can be discarded since it is an argument and not a definition at all.

We are thus presented with a philosophy where only concrete things are real. This implies that abstract things are not real. Hence, any arrangement or transition of arrangements, any order or consistency is not real. All reality would consist of the most minute physical entities in utter chaos. To avoid this absurdity by making such arrangements into concrete things is a fallacy called "reification". This fallacy may be given a seeming veracity by confusing the bodily processes of perception and reasoning – themselves dependent on the higher-level arrangements, and thus abstractions, of the body – with the abstraction being recognized.

The argument from the first definition suggests how this fallacy might be presented:

The Fallacy of Materialism

Premise A: The nervous system, including the brain, is part of the human body, which is physical; and

Premise B: Our knowledge is the result of physical stimuli being processed and stored in the brain.

Conclusion I: Knowledge is concrete.

Premises A and B are correct under the common usage of "physical". The problem with this argument is that the conclusion does not follow from the premises. First, our acquisition of knowledge is a process, as distinct from knowledge itself as the digestion of food is from the nutrients in our blood. Second, the physical includes both the concrete and the abstract. Third, a process need not impart its nature to what it processes. What does follow from the premises is therefore:

Conclusion II: Our knowledge is physically obtained and physically stored.

This latter conclusion does not even approach the less precise premise of materialism. That is, if we take the common usage of "physical material", this line of argument does not prove that knowledge is physical material. A moment's reflection shows that, while reflexes are physical material, knowledge is wholly abstract. A memory of a tree is stored in our brain, not the tree itself.

At this point of successive weakening, we get to the far less sweeping assertion that "the only reality is in material things and thinking about material things". Even so, this is a rather limited view of reality. One has to view people as material things in order to think about them, and then only in a physically-related way. This not only shows materialism at its most crass, it also shows itself incapable of any higher-level thought and crippled by an unimaginative empiricism. For all of its flaunted fervor for science, materialism of this ilk opposes both theoretical science and mathematics.

Yet were we to weaken the materialist strictures any further and admit second-order abstractions, would we be left with materialism after that relaxation? What reason would there be, moreover, in stopping there, rather than allowing higher-order abstractions until any materialist basis for knowledge is too remote to be of consequence? There is also no reason to suppose that a configuration of the brain corresponding to an abstract thought needs to be generated by physical stimulus or to be inherited as a physical reflex. If, instead, some abstract thoughts were innate, then that knowledge would not, in and of itself, have any concrete or physical basis, despite being stored physically.

Even without that last surmise, though, higher-order abstractions are sufficient to include the emotions and thus stories, plays and other imagined things which "atheists" and other materialists so readily dismiss and disparage. It can therefore be safely stated that materialism remains a fallacy, albeit a more clever one. For all of that, there may still be some apprehension of truth for which our intrepid "atheist" is clumsily reaching. Having dispensed with the more obvious fallacies and attempts to assume away anything which might allow a whisper of spirit or God, we next examine attempts to limit the discovery of truth through a false analogy with the courtroom.

The Material Court Fallacy

T he "atheist" or materialist will often attempt to equate the scientific process with sound reason and assert that the courts, by virtue of their use of various kinds of scientific evidence, are admitting the deficiency of evidence and the irrelevance of facts which are not physical. This confusion may be further aided by a third, legal, meaning of the word, "material", namely "relevance". Evidence or facts which are immaterial in the sense of not being physical would be immaterial in the legal sense when presented in the "scientific" or, more properly, "material court". This purported transformation of the legal system is then referenced in claims that any assertion about religion "wouldn't stand up in a modern court of law".

The fallacy here is that of a false analogy tinged

with arrogance. The scientific method is well adapted to ascertaining facts about physical things, but completely incompetent to prove motive or intent. Science may be employed more and more on the physical aspects of a case – as well it should – and can even obviate any emotional aspect in the verdict – when the law only requires proof of commission – but it can never prove motive or intent. For that, testimony about emotional facts is required. Since there are laws requiring proof of motive, since criminal law requires proof of criminal intent, since a criminal might cover their tracks well enough to require proof of motive with the remaining physical evidence and since sentencing often takes motive into account, it is safe to say that emotional facts will remain relevant even to the most modern court.

Along with the emotional facts comes a body of sound reasoning about them through centuries of law. The physical sciences have nothing to contribute there or to the related reasoning about incentives in the social sciences. The material court, like other materialist "improvements", are unnecessary limitations. There is no reason to dismiss a testimonial about emotions, for a criminal case, for resolution of conflicts or for sharing insights of the divine.

The broader issues of philosophy to which this analogy was applied nonetheless benefit from the aspect it suggests, however falsely. For the court analogy is one of the nature of proof, of what makes for a valid argument. We have just dispensed with a stricture which would have excluded a whole class of evidence from an argument, but we have not applied this analogy to what is the more germane direction of legal reasoning for an analysis of the nature of Existence, namely citing legal authority. For the nature of Existence is the ultimate authority under which all other existence is allowed, either directly or indirectly. Seeking the nature of Existence can then resemble appeals to higher and higher courts, or a child questioning "Why?"

It must be pointed out in this vein, that this question is not "How?" Neither the child nor the party bringing the suit are much interested in the mechanics but in the necessity of the result. Thus, the reason why the child has a stomachache after eating too much, too fast is that his body's digestive process is overloaded.

The reason why his body's digestive process is overloaded is that it can only digest so much food at a time and he ate faster than it could digest. The reason why his body's digestive process can only digest so much food at a time is because of the speed of the chemical reactions involved. The reason why those chemical reactions proceed at certain speeds is because of the molecular physics of those reactions. The reason why molecular physics is that way is because of a few other authorities until we reach one like "natural law" or "it just happens to be that way" or "God". At this ultimate authority, through a greater or lesser number of intermediate authorities, the question is answered.

That last answer, the one of the ultimate authority, also answers a question about the nature of Existence, of God, in a very rough outline. For these purposes, to see where the materialist position is in a philosophical landscape, we present the following categories of authority:

A. Deterministic. Everything is as it must be.

B. Arbitrary. Nothing is for sure.

C. Personal. Everything is as [Authority] lets it be.

Let us forgive the haughtiness of our materialist at the outset of this brief chapter and consider with him the question of the nature of God, to see in which category it is more reasonable to put that nature. With a conceptual rather than a personifying use of capitals, we may denote these categories as Fate, Chance and Will, respectively.

Fate, Chance or Will

T o help us decide which of these three kinds of authorities might reasonably be the kind of the ultimate authority, we first consider the implications of each being a higher authority than the others. No claim is made of anything more than a elementary analysis, but this territory is unfamiliar to materialists who call themselves "atheists". After exempting themselves from any metaphysical thoughts they cannot be expected to have a sophisticated or nuanced understanding of this philosophical field.

Let us then first consider if Fate is superior to Chance in authority. Random events then occur within some determined rules. This may seem reasonable but for the difficulty of where the randomness stops and determination takes over. One might also question whether Chance actually exists since the patterns of apparent randomness could be simply indications of our ignorance of lower-level mechanics which evenly distribute a large number of certain results. Fate would be complete in all particulars under its authority.

Next, if Chance is superior to Fate, then what we call natural law would be illusory. We just had a very good run of gravity and inertia, which could end at any moment. But that is not the only problem with Chance as God. The frequency of the random changes in Fate would be itself random, as would anything else. Reality could not be pinned down in any way under the authority of Chance.

Now, before we go any further, we need to make an important distinction. The introduction of Will into the discussion makes that distinction, between authority under another authority and authority within the context of another authority, important. For as long as we are talking about Fate and Chance, this is a distinction without an important difference. Whether three shows up on the die one-sixth of the time on average because the Law of Averages overrules randomness or because the shape of the die evenly distributes the certain but unknown outcomes, Fate replaces Chance in authority for either case. Similarly, as we have seen, randomly imposed rules – the mad king case – or rules set in a chaotic context – Roman law while Rome is being sacked – amount to the same thing: Chance replacing Fate in authority.

With Will, though, a choice can be made in a context without being made by the authority for that context. The soldier following the command of an officer is under the higher authority of his commander; his decision is made for him. A buyer at a market, however, makes his decision within the context of other authorities while still retaining that choice. The exercise of Will within the context set by another authority is yet the authority of that Will.

There is also a difference when Will is a higher authority. The rules of a game would be an example of Fate under the authority of the Will of the game creator or governing body. A roll of the dice to make a move under the rules of that game would be an example of Chance in a context of Fate. In the former case, Fate has no authority but from the superior authority of the Will. In the latter case, Chance keeps its authority within its context.

The cases involving Will are therefore:

1. Chance superior to Will. The authority of Will is illusory since all apparent decisions are random.

2. Fate superior to Will. The authority of Will is illusory since all apparent decisions are determined.

3. Will superior to Chance. The authority of Chance is illusory since all apparent randomness is by the choice of Will.

4. Will superior to Fate. The authority of Fate is illusory since all apparent consistency is by the choice of Will.

5. Will superior to Will. The authority of the subordinate Will is illusory since all apparent choices by the subordinate Will

are, in fact, choices by the superior Will.

6. Chance set in a context of Will. Chance retains its authority in the context set by Will.

7. Fate set in a context of Will. Fate retains its authority in the context set by Will.

8. Will set in a context of Chance. Will retains its authority in the context set by Chance.

9. Will set in a context of Fate. Will retains its authority in the context set by Fate.

10. Will set in a context of another Will. Will retains its authority in the context set by that other Will.

It should be clear that, if the authority of Chance was ultimate, there would be complete chaos, far beyond what we could imagine in our worst nightmare or most fantastic dream. That leaves Fate and Will as candidates for ultimate authority. Materialists form one group favoring Fate but they are not alone; they are joined by Calvinists and many others as equally devout. And, of course, there are many who hold Will to be the ultimate authority. As the utter chaos of Chance as the ultimate authority is not in anyone's experience, so each would favor Will or Fate as one or the other is more consistent with their own experience or their view of that experience.

Nonetheless, there are some problematic views relative to the contexts being set or not by the ultimate authority. Some expect natural law to be contravened by Will at the drop of a hat, while others suppose that Will is incapable of the consistency of Fate. The creativity of Will, which makes the setting of contexts for other authorities believable, is not required of Fate. On the other hand, some think that creativity does not reside in lesser Wills.

Let us put these matters in less theoretical terms. Materialists would, we expect, believe reality is one big machine and, if we knew all of the inputs, we could determine all of the outputs. The modern strain maps this model down to the person, who is thus fated to do what they will do and is deluded if they think they have a choice. Earlier strains allowed for personal exceptions of choice within their own contexts, without explaining how the machine manufactured those contexts or kept more volatile persons from breaching them or from hacking into the code of the universe, destroying reality. Perhaps the prospect of Matter-dammerung urged a more limited model of humanity. Be that as it may, mechanistic fatalism is the fashion of the day for these materialists.

The alternative view, missing from the machine instructions of the materialists, is that the ultimate authority is a Will, also called the Great Spirit, Love, God and a host of other names, each reflecting some aspect of the nature of Existence; that Fate, or natural Law, exists by the decision of that Will, is upheld by the authority of that Will and forms the context for the Wills of each person; and that the Will of each person, for lack of a more acceptable word, is their soul. In this view, knowledge of the natural context is a celebration of the Great Spirit which created it. In this view, each person is creative and is akin to God because they are a

Will. In this view, all Will is Love, the sharing of Will which multiplies it, filling the natural context with creative fruitfulness.

Between these two views, one of barren slavery to fate, the other bearing the fruits of freedom, there is but little choice. Attempts to dismiss the latter as unreal by insisting on concrete evidence of the soul or God, are no more valid than dismissing $2 + 2 = 4$ as unreal until concrete evidence can be furnished of the numbers 2 and 4, of the addition operator and of the equality relation. In the last analysis, some people refuse to be convinced of the obvious.

We have proceeded as far as we can with a name that charitably casts the philosophy of modern atheism. However, materialism neither describes nor can it be responsible for what has been issuing from that quarter. On the other hand, words like "anti-religious" are as fallacious as "atheist" while bearing the disadvantage of not being their self-chosen moniker. Thus, we revert to using the oxymoron "atheist" as we turn to the fallacies of the flaws they point out in others. Though these flaws are falsely attributed to religion and the fallacies not recognized, the atheists have performed a service in bringing these matters to the attention of the public. Perhaps, we can join together in ridding humanity of these scourges.

The Fallacy of Morality

uch of the recent criticism of "religion" by atheists centers around the public condemnation of their private lives by certain individuals who claim to speak for their religion. Usually, these individuals are new adherents to a faith they do not understand, being only aware that they felt guilty before and do not feel guilty now. As newly reformed people, they mistake their reformation for a license to condemn, despite any Scripture passages to the contrary.

There will always be those who will exploit these fragile people for their own personal and political gain, even doing so under the name of religion. That exploitation is, sad to say, a profitable business, made even more profitable by the air-time the profits can buy.

Large buildings are erected. Large congregations are assembled. A few good works are done. The stage is set to send forth crowds of condemners, a plurality aspiring to be a majority sitting in moral judgment of "sinners".

All the while, the true religion, in humble houses of worship, works mercy untelevised. Maybe some of their number are sick and, staying home, are made sicker still by watching a perversion of their faith they would not have seen when healthy. They think of "judge not, that you be not judged", saddened and helpless before the powers of this world.

Moral judgment is opposed by religion, not by Scripture passages only, but for a more fundamental reason. Living as Wills in community, experiencing an all-embracing Loving Will in prayer, people of faith act in that Will of Love. Morality is not necessary for them. Indeed, morality destroys the communities of faith, poisoning them with condemnation and pride, thereby separating them from the Will and Love of God.

Yet, religion is slandered and hands outstretched in comfort are pushed away. More sadly still, those who are condemned by pretend religion seek out their own morality, to condemn true religion, instead. In so doing, they are not only rude and obnoxious to the innocent, but fall into the same error as their tormentors.

For if Fate is the ultimate authority and rules over all, so that we are not Wills but machines, then our actions are inevitable. We cannot change them to suit the dictates of any system of ethics. Moral judgment has no grounds in this case. We are all innocent by reason of Fate.

If we are Wills, set in a context of Fate by Fate, then morality is either individual, based on each Will, or universal, based on a constant moral code of Fate. If morality is individual, the moral code is enacted by the individual and does not apply to others. This is not morality at all, but the application of Will.

If there is a constant moral code of Fate, then it is always enforced by Fate. If we think that something is a natural law and it is not enforced in all cases, then we consider ourselves mistaken; the same would apply for moral law. The lightning bolt always strikes you on every infraction. In this case, also, there is no morality, only prudence.

The cases where Will is the ultimate authority, our Will under the authority of the supreme Will and our Will set in a context of Fate by the supreme Will, also show that morality is nonsense. If every thought is directed by God, there can be no culpability in our acts coming from those thoughts. If we are free Wills and the moral code is part of the context of Fate, morality would consist of slavish adherence to the construct over getting to know the constructor. The fallacy is taking a mere moral code to be the basis of a judgment of Will and in presuming that judgment would even be desired by a supreme Will. It is Man that desires judgment and sacrifice, not God.

Morality, though fallacious, does confer power and that is what makes it dangerous. There are moral truths and those who know some of them, and are keen to exploit the prestige that knowledge confers, may use their prestige to proclaim politically expedient rules as moral truth. This is another dynamic the atheists rightly criticize, as we see in the next fallacy.

The Fallacy of Expert Opinion

A solitary figure ascends a rostrum as a hushed crowd gazes in rapt attention from their seats in the darkened auditorium. As he begins to speak, the people prepare to soak in every word. These will be their thoughts for the coming week. These will be the words they share with those at work. These are the beliefs they will hold fast despite all who might contradict them.

And such is the image presented by the atheists of the life of the faithful. Never mind that most worship services are held in the day. Never mind that the words of the preacher, the rabbi or the mullah interpret older writings that most of the faithful have heard before, have heard interpreted before, have they themselves thought about. Never mind that the worshipers listen in politeness during the service, to disagree in the social hour afterward. Never mind that there is far more to their services than the opinions of the religious experts. The atheists will cling to this image no matter how often or how pointedly their religious friends contradict them. Such friends are always exceptions to the rule.

Of course, the religious friends are the rule of actual religion and the televised "evangelism" is some other rule. A similar scene shows what that other rule is. The acceptance speeches at political conventions are made in just the scene described. The post-convention certainty about everything their political experts told them, despite all contradiction in logic and fact, is far more evident than even the remembrance of last week's sermon by the parishioners. Therein lies the similarity: both convention and evangelism shows are mass conversion events. The one converts supporters of other candidates into rabid followers of the party nominee; the other converts the non-religious into rabid followers of the religion being evangelized.

The fresh converts in both cases do not know much about their new cause. They are wholly dependent on expert opinion for what to think, what to do and how to vote. Those who have lived their cause for some time do not have this disability. If someone were to claim about longtime party members what atheists claim about religious people, they would get the same eye rolls as religious people give the atheists. In fact, that has been happening recently in the party rhetoric, each side charging the other with being unthinking fools.

If everyone would just step back a little, though, and see what is happening, they would realize that these errors only occur with those who stop thinking critically when presented with expert opinion. For though that expertise may be initially recognized with great validity among those capable of validating it, if no one critically examines their work, there will eventually be no one who can validate. This may happen even among several working in a field, for they might coalesce into a school of thought with common assumptions and prejudices.

Another aspect of the fallacy of expert opinion is what is also known as the fallacy of "appeal to authority". That is where the reputation of the expert in one field is transferred to another where they do not have expertise. The classic case of this is that of Galileo being tried for heresy on the basis of experts in Biblical studies using their authority in the political hierarchy of the Roman Church to claim expertise in astronomy. Yet there are plenty of other cases without religious association where political and academic authority in one discipline is used to claim expertise other areas, often with disastrous results. A current example is that of climate experts claiming, for their proposed remedy of global warming, expertise in economics and accusing economists who dispute their proposal of being science deniers. A sane, rational discussion would ensue on all matters if expert opinion was not allowed to end debate.

Still, that is not likely to happen as long as each thought is colored by its partisan implications, so that each side brings in *their* experts to end the debate *their* way. For even the well-thought and critically-thinking person will surrender their mind to blind acceptance of all sorts of nonsense once they have allowed it to be infected with partisan politics. The massive loss of life from this social disease, in wars throughout history, has been the great tragedy of mankind. Though somewhat obliquely, atheism has reminded us of this key truth.

The Fallacy of Partisan Politics

T he story, as the atheists tell it, is that religion is responsible for all the wars, for all the barbarism and for all the strife in the world. That, of course, is utter nonsense. War is a political institution, not a religious one. One need only look at the many pacifist sects throughout the religious landscape to find proof of this fact.

The confusion for the atheists on this point is between the administration of the religious institutions and the religion itself. It is a common confusion in its general form, as in the conflating of the people with their government. For as long as a community is small, the practice of a communal faith and the workings of common action are each identical with their administration.

However, once their religious and civic spheres start to expand into neighboring towns and further, religious and civic administrations are first separated from the people's faith and polity and then become more remote. As they become more remote, these administrations become more powerful and more willing to exert that power. The exertion of power by distant administrations is then felt by the local communities, so that their local practices are threatened. Instead of being able to go their own way, these communities are forced to defend their way by imposing it on others. Those communities whose local ways are in agreement with each other form alliances for this purpose, installing in the distant administrations politicians favorable to their common ways, their partisan ways. Partisan politics is born.

As the scope of the political parties in religious and civic administration expands, the conflicts become more intense and the original local ways are forgotten. There might be great similarities in civic and religious life between two towns, but residents are made to fear that they will become Muslims if they are Catholics, or Democrats if they are Republicans, on the ascendancy of the opposite party. To ensure that their party does not lose control or that it gains it, campaigns are waged, sometimes metaphorically and sometimes not. Despite the facade of civilization, wars break out and the world descends into barbarism.

What allows this loss of humanity is the loss of reason coming from the fallacy of partisan politics. One may hope that this fallacy is subtle, that there is some stubborn puzzle which stands in the way of peace, but it is as simple as it is deadly: One's own party is good and the other party is evil. Any seeming finesse or ingenuity in the presentation of this simplistic view, say in impugning the intelligence of those in the opposite party, is a pastiche on its banal morality. And it is that banal morality which makes partisan politics so deadly. If the other party is evil, its adherents do not deserve to live and war is justified.

When we realize this awful truth, it becomes our duty to do what we can to rid the world of the scourge of partisan politics. We should not despair of making a contribution, for the source of partisan politics is in allowing remote administration of our intimate lives. If we each help re-build our local communities and make them self-reliant in the practice of faith and civics, we sap the power of the political parties in both pursuits. And if we are diligent in building our institutions in a federal manner, never intruding on more local rule, we can help to build a world in peace.

Conclusion

H aving setting matters straight, as best I know how, so that there can be some meaningful and constructive rapport between atheists and religious people toward a more loving and peaceful world, there does not seem much more to say than to urge us all to get to it. Anything further is too much of a delay.